the Recipes of
Madison County

Published 1995 by Oxmoor House, Inc.
Book Division of Southern Progress Corporation
P.O. Box 2463, Birmingham, Alabama 35201

©1995 by Jane M. Hemminger and Courtney A. Work

Library of Congress Catalog Card Number: 95-70251
ISBN: 0-8487-1506-3
Manufactured in the United States of America
First Printing 1995

Editor-in-Chief: Nancy Fitzpatrick Wyatt
Senior Editor, Editorial Services: Olivia Kindig Wells
Art Director: James Boone

The Recipes of Madison County

Senior Foods Editor: Susan Carlisle Payne
Foods Editors: Julie Fisher, Deborah Garrison Lowery
Copy Editor: Keri Bradford Anderson
Editorial Assistant: Alison Rich Lewis
Food Consultant: Lynn Lloyd
Production and Distribution Director: Phillip Lee
Production Manager: Gail H. Morris
Associate Production Manager: Theresa L. Beste
Production Assistant: Marianne Jordan Wilson

This book was developed in cooperation with the Goddard Book Group
of Chicago.

the Recipes of
Madison County

Written and Illustrated by
Jane M. Hemminger and Courtney A. Work

Oxmoor
House.

Acknowledgments

In the fall of 1994 we were given the opportunity to work on the movie *The Bridges of Madison County*. Channing Work, Courtney's brother and the movie's Production Assistant, was asked to find Prop Caterers for the movie. That fortunate connection along with a great deal of food and catering experience got us hired. Channing, we're very grateful.

We're also appreciative of the time given to us by the Prop Master, Eddie Aiona. The information relating to each scene helped us provide the appropriate menu suggestions. His explanation of set up, prop placement, and filming techniques created visual images for our preparations.

Thanks to Pat Work, Ellen Morgan, Esther Ronan, Virginia Traxler, Mary Stines, and Marjorie Hemminger for providing our unique advantage of growing up on Midwestern meals. Without family inspiration we couldn't have produced this book.

A very special thank you to Connie Goddard, our agent, for supporting our creative ideas. Without her help this book would have remained only an idea. Also to Bill Graham for all his hard work and sound advice. And to Annabel Wimer for her enthusiasm in seeing our vision of this book and helping make it possible.

To Lynne Lynch for her wonderful care of our children.

And last to our husbands, Tom and David, who have been there to take care of Grover and Grady, Will and Ellen. We love you . . . and your huts in Mexico are waiting for you.

Contents

Introduction

⌒⟡⌒

For Francesca Johnson and Robert Kincaid, a glass of iced tea starts it all.

She offers. He accepts. And from that moment on, the lives of an Iowa housewife and an adventurous photographer are passionately intertwined in the movie *The Bridges of Madison County*. Funny how an offering so simple—a glass of tea—could open the floodgate to a lifetime of feelings.

However, we didn't even need an offer of iced tea to accept the invitation to serve as food advisers and prop caterers for filming *The Bridges of Madison County*. We had the opportunity to work on the set of the movie, which was filmed near our homes, because we know the culinary habits of Iowans and could deliver the food from our kitchen in Des Moines.

Each time the prop master explained the important role food would play in the movie, we could relate it to a time and place when food served a similar role in our own lives. We began to realize the strong part food plays in strengthening the bonds of intimacy in all relationships . . . and the idea for this cookbook took root.

The simple offering of food nurtures romance.

For centuries, the stages of a romantic relationship have revolved around food—from a first-date dinner to an impromptu picnic to cooking for each other on a regular basis. Eating together offers a subtle way to build intimacy into a relationship. Romance blossoms for Francesca and Robert over candlelight and wildflowers.

Food is often the first step in developing friendships.

A simple Apple Brown Betty was the key to many friendships we developed on the movie set. We made that classic American dessert for the scene in which Madge drops by to gossip with Francesca. Bad weather delayed the filming on the day the scene was to be shot, so we became friends with many of the crew members when we offered . . . and they downed . . . 12 pounds of Apple Brown Betty! In the same way, Francesca builds a friendship with Lucy Redfield after delivering a simple homemade cake.

Food sparks fond memories in family relationships.

Especially within families, our bonds become tighter as family members repeat food traditions that create more memories, and then pass both on to the next generation. A holiday tradition of baking and delivering Apricot Coffee Crescents, for example, is but one way generations can develop and maintain the closeness of family.

Even the routine Johnson family meals in the movie provide a sense of security and comfort by the very nature of their familiarity. Not much said, but the bonds of dependency and responsibility for each other seem strengthened just by the act of eating the same familiar foods together. It's that sense of responsibility that prevents Francesca from leaving her husband and children to follow her passionate desire to be with Robert.

Food is also a physical expression of caring and compassion.

Food is a way of saying, "You're special in my life." People commonly take food to celebrate a birth, comfort the bereaved, and express concern for the sick. That unexpected pot of chicken soup from a friend feeds the soul as much as it nourishes the body.

These are the roles food plays for people everywhere, not just in rural Madison County, Iowa.

Although we often cook and eat differently today than we did in the 1960s, many times we long to return to the "comfort foods" of our childhood.

On the pages that follow we give you the actual 1960s-style recipes that Francesca serves in the movie to her family, to Robert, and to her friends. We reached into our family files for these recipes, and we still serve them to our own families when the need arises for flavors from our memories.

Along with the 1960s favorites, we've included in this book menus and recipes that reflect today's quicker and trendier style of cooking. That's because even though today's lifestyle is faster paced, it doesn't change our desire to use food as an expression of love. Also included in this book, much like the props in the movie, are suggestions to create an environment that's just as special as the food. The perfect meal won't achieve its goal without appropriate surroundings—dim the lights for romance, brighten up the table for family gatherings, jazz up the music for entertaining friends. Consider these suggestions as starting points to your own creativity.

The essential element is the amount of time you linger over food.

Use this time to let passions of a relationship develop naturally. Friend to friend. Mother to daughter. Neighbor to neighbor. Man to woman.

It could all start with a glass of iced tea . . .

Jane and Courtney

Nurturing the Family

Dinner Before Departing

Setting the Mood

Johnson farmhouse kitchen
Everyday dishes
Paper napkins
Cast-iron skillet
Radio in background

∾

Menu

Skillet-Grilled Sausages
Scalloped Iowa Corn
American Fries
Cottage Cheese
Sliced White Bread
Fresh Apple Pie

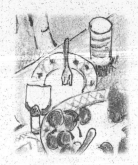

*O*ur first glimpse of the Johnson family, scurrying for a meal before they leave for the fair, reveals one issue that taxes this family and so many others. There's so much to do, and so little time. Even so, Francesca manages to get a hearty, nourishing meat-and-potatoes meal on the table before the family's departure. But as mothers so often feel, her efforts hardly seem appreciated. Time for meaningful, soul-nurturing conversation will have to come later.

Skillet-Grilled Sausages

Vegetable cooking spray
1½   pounds link turkey kielbasa (1 inch thick)
2   tablespoons water
Dijon mustard

Spray a large cast-iron or nonstick skillet with cooking spray; heat over medium heat. Cut sausages diagonally into 2-inch sections. Place sausages in skillet, and sauté until browned. Add water; cover and simmer over low heat 8 to 10 minutes or until thoroughly heated. Serve on a platter with Dijon mustard for dipping. Yield: 4 to 6 servings.

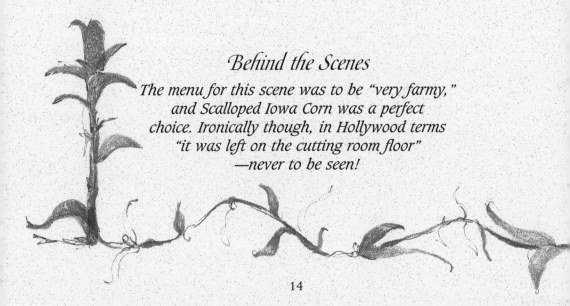

Behind the Scenes

The menu for this scene was to be "very farmy,"
and Scalloped Iowa Corn was a perfect
choice. Ironically though, in Hollywood terms
"it was left on the cutting room floor"
—never to be seen!

Scalloped Iowa Corn

6   to 8 ears sweet yellow corn
1⅔   cups milk
1   tablespoon sugar
¼   cup butter or margarine, divided
2   tablespoons all-purpose flour
½   teaspoon salt
¼   teaspoon paprika
⅛   teaspoon pepper
1   large egg, lightly beaten
¼   cup chopped onion
¾   cup crushed saltine crackers (about 20 crackers)

Slice enough corn from cobs to yield 2 cups, scraping cobs well to remove milk from cobs. Combine corn, 1⅔ cups milk, and sugar in a saucepan. Bring almost to a boil over medium heat; reduce heat, and simmer 5 minutes, stirring often. Drain corn, reserving liquid.

Melt 2 tablespoons butter in a heavy saucepan over low heat; add flour, stirring until smooth. Cook 1 minute, stirring constantly. Gradually add reserved corn liquid; cook over medium heat, stirring constantly, until mixture is thickened and bubbly. Remove from heat. Stir in corn, salt, paprika, pepper, egg, and onion. Set aside.

Melt remaining 2 tablespoons butter in a small skillet; remove from heat. Stir cracker crumbs into butter. Stir ½ cup of crumb mixture into corn mixture; spoon corn mixture into a deep, greased 1½-quart casserole dish. Sprinkle remaining crumb mixture over top. Bake, uncovered, at 350° for 20 to 25 minutes or until lightly browned. Yield: 4 servings.

American Fries

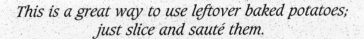

*This is a great way to use leftover baked potatoes;
just slice and sauté them.*

3	medium baking potatoes
2	tablespoons vegetable oil
½	cup chopped onion
½	cup chopped green pepper
½	cup chopped sweet red pepper
½	teaspoon salt
¼	teaspoon pepper
¼	teaspoon garlic powder

Place whole potatoes in a large saucepan, and cover with water.
Bring water to a boil; cover and cook potatoes 10 minutes or
until partially cooked. Drain potatoes, and slice ¼-inch thick; do
not peel.

 Heat oil in a large skillet. Add sliced potatoes and onion
to skillet, and cook 5 minutes or until potatoes are browned,
turning potatoes to brown on both sides. Add green and red
peppers, salt, pepper, and garlic powder. Cover and cook 3 to 5
minutes or until potatoes are done. Serve immediately. Yield:
4 servings.

Fresh Apple Pie

3	cups plus 1 tablespoon all-purpose flour, divided
1	teaspoon salt, divided
1	teaspoon ground cinnamon, divided
1½	cups shortening
1	large egg
1	teaspoon white vinegar
¼	cup plus 2 tablespoons milk, divided
3	cups peeled, sliced cooking apples (6 to 8)
2	teaspoons lemon juice
¼	teaspoon ground nutmeg
1	cup plus 1 tablespoon sugar, divided
2	tablespoons butter or margarine

Combine 3 cups flour, ½ teaspoon salt, and ¼ teaspoon cinnamon. Cut shortening into flour mixture until mixture resembles crumbs. Combine egg, vinegar, and ¼ cup plus 1 tablespoon milk; stir into flour mixture. Chill 2 hours. Roll half of pastry to ⅛-inch thickness on a heavily floured surface; keep remaining half refrigerated. Place pastry in a 9-inch pieplate.

Combine apples, remaining 1 tablespoon flour, remaining ½ teaspoon salt, remaining ¾ teaspoon cinnamon, lemon juice, nutmeg, and 1 cup sugar. Pour into crust. Dot apples with butter.

Roll remaining pastry to ⅛-inch thickness; transfer to pie. Trim pastry; seal and flute edges. Cut slits in top crust. Brush crust with remaining 1 tablespoon milk. Sprinkle with remaining 1 tablespoon sugar. Bake at 425° for 15 minutes; reduce heat to 350°, and bake 25 minutes or until apples test done. Cover with foil if pie browns too quickly. Yield: one 9-inch pie.

A Meal for Relaxing

Setting the Mood

Family room in front of a fire if serving spinach soup
Porch or patio if serving gazpacho
Large soup bowls
Bright place mats and napkins
Bread board
Deck of cards

~~~

Menu

Spinach-Provolone Soup or
Lobster Gazpacho
Orange-Avocado Salad
with Poppy Seed Dressing
Warm Sourdough Bread

*A*s we saw in that first movie meal for family, cooking can be quite a production, so it's nice to have menus and recipes that aren't. When the weekend rolls around, make it a priority to have casual meals without a lot of fuss. All of these recipes are quick to make and can be partially or totally made ahead. This lets you take the day as it comes and spend time with your family rather than in the kitchen. It's time, now, to nourish their souls.

Spinach-Provolone Soup

1	(10-ounce) package frozen chopped spinach, thawed and undrained
½	cup chopped onion
½	cup diced carrot
½	cup sliced celery
¼	cup diced sweet red pepper
3	tablespoons butter or margarine, melted
3	tablespoons all-purpose flour
3	cups skim or low-fat milk
1	cup chicken broth
1	teaspoon salt
¼	teaspoon ground nutmeg
⅛	teaspoon lemon-pepper seasoning
¾	cup (3 ounces) shredded provolone cheese
4	slices bacon, cooked and crumbled

Puree spinach in a food processor.

Sauté onion, carrot, celery, and red pepper in butter in a large, heavy saucepan. Add flour, stirring until smooth. Cook, stirring constantly, 2 minutes. Gradually add milk and chicken broth; cook over medium heat, stirring constantly, until mixture is thickened and bubbly. Stir in spinach, salt, nutmeg, and lemon-pepper. Cook until thoroughly heated. Sprinkle each serving evenly with provolone cheese and crumbled bacon. Yield: 4 servings.

Lobster Gazpacho

Don't hesitate to change the lobster to any seafood—fresh crabmeat, shrimp, and scallops are excellent alternatives.

6	medium tomatoes, peeled and chopped
½	cup chopped purple or sweet white onion
1	large cucumber, peeled and chopped
1	green pepper, chopped
2	cups fresh or canned tomato juice
1	clove garlic, crushed
1	tablespoon paprika
1	tablespoon chopped fresh parsley
2	teaspoons sugar
1½	teaspoons ground cumin
½	teaspoon salt
¼	teaspoon pepper
2	teaspoons red wine vinegar
¼	cup olive oil
8	drops of hot sauce
8	ounces cooked lobster tail, sliced
¼	cup sour cream or plain yogurt
1	tablespoon chopped fresh parsley

Combine first 15 ingredients in a large bowl. Cover and chill at least 4 hours (mixture will be thick and chunky). Stir in lobster slices just before serving. Serve with a garnish of sour cream and parsley. Yield: 4 servings.

Orange-Avocado Salad

—⁓—

2   heads Bibb lettuce, torn into bite-size pieces
1   (8-ounce) can mandarin oranges, drained
1   avocado
¼   cup diced purple onion
4   fresh mushrooms, sliced
¼   cup sunflower kernels, toasted
¼   cup freshly grated Parmesan cheese (optional)
Poppy Seed Dressing

Line each salad plate with lettuce; top with oranges. Peel and slice avocado, fanning 3 slices onto each plate. Sprinkle salads evenly with onion, mushrooms, sunflower kernels, and, if desired, cheese. Top with Poppy Seed Dressing. Yield: 4 servings.

Poppy Seed Dressing

¼   cup olive oil
¼   cup cider vinegar
2   tablespoons sugar
1   teaspoon poppy seeds
2   teaspoons lime juice
¼   teaspoon dry mustard
¼   teaspoon Worcestershire sauce

Combine all ingredients in a jar; cover tightly, and shake vigorously. Chill. Yield: ½ cup.

Sparking a Relationship

Spur-of-the-Moment Menu

Setting the Mood

Farmhouse kitchen
Large tea pitcher
Yellow checked glasses
Blue field flowers
Vegetables from the garden
Everyday dishes
Brandy snifters

Menu

Iced Tea
Fresh Vegetable Spaghetti
Steamed Fresh Carrots
Breadsticks
Mocha Fudge Brownie Bites
Coffee   Brandy

*W*ithout Francesca's hesitant but determined invitation to Robert for iced tea, their relationship may never have developed. And that initial invitation leads to an evening of food-related offers. There is dinner, relatively easy to throw together with Robert's eagerness to help; then coffee, and later brandy—all meant to prolong the departure of her fascinating new acquaintance.

Fresh Vegetable Spaghetti

½   pound ground turkey breast or turkey sausage
½   onion, chopped
1   clove garlic, minced
½   (6-ounce) can tomato paste
1   (8-ounce) can tomato sauce
½   (14½-ounce) can diced tomatoes
2   tablespoons shredded Cheddar cheese
1   tablespoon chopped fresh parsley
1½   teaspoons sugar
½   teaspoon dried basil
½   teaspoon dried oregano
4   drops of hot sauce
Dash of ground thyme
⅓   cup chopped green pepper
1   tomato, chopped
1½   cups sliced fresh mushrooms
Hot cooked spaghetti or angel hair pasta

Brown turkey, onion, and garlic in a large, heavy saucepan over medium heat, stirring to crumble meat. Add tomato paste and next 9 ingredients; cover and simmer on medium-low heat 15 to 20 minutes, stirring occasionally. Add green pepper, tomato, and mushrooms, and cook 5 minutes or until thoroughly heated. Serve over spaghetti. Yield: about 3 cups sauce.

Mocha Fudge Brownie Bites

1	cup (6 ounces) semisweet chocolate morsels
¼	cup butter or margarine
1	tablespoon instant coffee granules
1	large egg
1	large egg yolk
⅔	cup all-purpose flour
½	cup sugar
⅛	teaspoon baking soda
1	tablespoon coffee-flavored liqueur
1	teaspoon vanilla extract

Powdered sugar

Combine chocolate and butter in a medium-size, heavy saucepan; cook over low heat, stirring constantly, until melted. Add coffee granules, egg, and egg yolk; stir until blended. Stir in flour, sugar, baking soda, coffee-flavored liqueur, and vanilla. Pour into a lightly greased 8-inch square pan. Bake at 350° for 20 to 25 minutes or until a wooden pick inserted in center comes out clean. Cool on a wire rack. Sprinkle with powdered sugar, and cut into bite-size pieces. Yield: 49 squares.

A Meal Meant for Lingering

Setting the Mood

Dining room
Linens—a dark color will set off this menu
Good dishes
Dim lights
Soft music
Wine
Wildflowers
Good conversation

Menu

White Lasagna
Vegetables with Lemon Sauce
Hot French Bread
Fruit Trifle
Wine   Coffee

*W*e are all far more complex than a first intro-
duction can reveal. Only through spending
quality time with someone can personal attrib-
utes . . . and opportunities . . . be discovered.
Often these discoveries are made during an
intimate meal. Use this time to its fullest,
encouraging conversation and including your
companion in as much food preparation as
possible. Pour that first glass of wine while
still in the kitchen, and let the evening take
you where it will.

White Lasagna

~~~~~

1	tablespoon butter or margarine
1½	tablespoons all-purpose flour
¾	cup milk
¼	cup chicken broth
1	clove garlic, minced
⅛	teaspoon white pepper
½	medium onion, sliced into thin strips
2	cups sliced fresh mushrooms
1	tablespoon olive oil
1	(14½-ounce) can artichoke hearts, drained and chopped
8	lasagna noodles, cooked, drained, and cut into thirds
½	cup (2 ounces) shredded mozzarella cheese, divided
1	cup finely grated fresh Parmesan cheese, divided

Melt butter in a saucepan; stir in flour. Cook 1 minute, stirring constantly. Gradually add milk and broth; cook, stirring constantly, until mixture is thickened. Stir in garlic and pepper. Sauté onion and mushrooms in oil; stir in artichokes. Set aside.

Spread 1½ teaspoons white sauce into 4 greased (2-cup) casseroles. Place 2 pieces of noodles in each dish. Top each with 1 tablespoon white sauce, 2 tablespoons artichoke mixture, 1 tablespoon mozzarella, and 2 tablespoons Parmesan. Top each evenly using half of noodles, 2 tablespoons white sauce, remaining artichoke mixture, and remaining mozzarella. Sprinkle 1 tablespoon Parmesan on each. Top evenly with final layers of noodles, white sauce, and remaining ¼ cup Parmesan. Cover with foil; bake at 375° for 15 minutes. Remove foil, and bake 10 minutes or until lightly browned. Freezes well. Yield: 4 servings.

Vegetables with Lemon Sauce

This is a light and refreshing accompaniment for the pasta dish in this menu or any other rich entrée.

½   cup cauliflower flowerettes
⅓   cup sliced carrot
½   cup broccoli flowerettes
¼   cup julienne-sliced sweet red pepper
¼   cup julienne-sliced sweet yellow pepper
½   cup chicken broth
1½ teaspoons cornstarch
1½ teaspoons water
2   teaspoons butter or margarine
2   teaspoons lemon juice
1   tablespoon chopped fresh parsley
1   teaspoon sliced green onion
Dash of white pepper
Dash of seasoned salt

Combine cauliflower and carrot in a steamer basket over boiling water. Cover and steam vegetables 5 to 7 minutes. Add broccoli and red and yellow peppers; steam another 6 to 8 minutes or until crisp-tender. Drain.

Meanwhile, heat chicken broth in a small saucepan. Combine cornstarch and water, stirring until blended; add to broth, stirring constantly, until smooth and thickened. Add butter, lemon juice, parsley, green onion, pepper, and seasoned salt; cook 1 minute. Drizzle lemon sauce over vegetables just before serving. Yield: 2 servings.

Fruit Trifle

Here's a simple yet elegant finish.

1   (8-ounce) carton vanilla yogurt
1   teaspoon superfine sugar
4   medium kiwifruit, peeled and sliced
1   cup fresh blueberries
1   cup fresh raspberries
4   amaretto cookies or any other crisp wafer-style cookie,
       crushed
2   sprigs fresh mint

Combine yogurt and sugar. Line bottom and sides of two stemmed sherbet glasses with kiwifruit. Top with a heaping tablespoon of yogurt, followed by blueberries. Top blueberries with a heaping tablespoon of yogurt, followed by raspberries. Top raspberries with remaining yogurt. Sprinkle with cookie crumbs. Garnish with mint sprigs. Yield: 2 servings.

Just Between Two

A Passionate Evening

Setting the Mood

Farmhouse kitchen
Flowers in a jelly jar
Blues on the radio
Ranier beer
Summer breeze

～～

Menu

Wild Rice-Stuffed Green Peppers
Tossed Garden Salad with
Creamy Vinaigrette
French Bread
Strawberries and Nectarines with Cream
Pecan Dreams

*F*ood continues to play a key role in building the relationship between Francesca and Robert when she tacks a dinner invitation on the Roseman Bridge for Robert. Green peppers with wild rice stuffing were a perfect choice for this meal; subtly they symbolize the contrast between the heaviness of Francesca's everyday life and the freshness of her encounter with Robert. The simplicity of Francesca's stuffed peppers, a jelly jar of flowers, and blues on the radio set just the right mood for this steamy evening.

Wild Rice-Stuffed Green Peppers

1/3	cup chopped onion
1	clove garlic, minced
1	tablespoon butter or margarine, melted
1 1/2	cups beef broth
3/4	cup long-grain, brown, and wild rice blend
1/3	cup sliced celery
1/4	cup finely chopped carrot
1	(14 1/2-ounce) can diced tomatoes, undrained
1	cup sliced fresh mushrooms
1/2	cup chopped zucchini
2	tablespoons chopped fresh parsley
1/4	teaspoon dried basil
1/8	to 1/4 teaspoon ground thyme
2	large green peppers, stem ends sliced off
1	to 2 tablespoons tomato juice (optional)
1/4	cup grated fresh Parmesan cheese

Sauté onion and garlic in butter in a large saucepan until tender. Add broth, rice, celery, and carrot. Bring to a boil; cover, reduce heat, and simmer 25 minutes or until rice is almost done. Remove from heat; stir in tomatoes and next 5 ingredients.

Place peppers in a saucepan; cover with water. Bring to a boil; cook 3 minutes or until crisp-tender. Drain; stuff with rice mixture. Place peppers in a 1 1/2-quart greased casserole; spoon any extra rice around peppers. Cover with foil; bake at 350° for 25 minutes or until tender, basting with tomato juice after 15 minutes if mixture seems dry. When almost done, remove foil, and top with Parmesan; bake 5 more minutes. Yield: 2 servings.

Tossed Garden Salad

3   cups loosely packed mixed salad greens
¼   cup diced cucumber
¼   cup cauliflower flowerettes
2   tablespoons chopped purple onion
1   radish, diced
Creamy Vinaigrette
¼   cup seasoned croutons
2   slices bacon, cooked and crumbled
2   Roma tomatoes, quartered

Combine first 5 ingredients; toss with Creamy Vinaigrette, and spoon onto salad plates. Sprinkle with croutons and bacon. Garnish with tomato quarters. Yield: 2 servings.

Creamy Vinaigrette

3   tablespoons regular or low-fat sour cream
3   tablespoons olive oil
3   tablespoons wine vinegar
1   tablespoon sugar
½   teaspoon dried basil
½   teaspoon dried parsley flakes
½   teaspoon dried oregano
1   clove garlic, minced

Combine all ingredients in a jar; cover tightly, and shake vigorously. Yield: ½ cup.

Strawberries and Nectarines with Cream

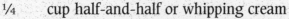

¼   cup half-and-half or whipping cream
1   tablespoon superfine sugar
2   teaspoons port wine or Grand Marnier
1   pint fresh strawberries, stemmed and halved
2   nectarines, cubed
Mint leaves

Combine half-and-half, sugar, and port wine; cover mixture, and chill 1 hour.

Combine strawberries and nectarines; spoon into serving dishes or wine glasses. Drizzle cream mixture over fruit, and garnish with mint leaves. Yield: 2 servings.

Pecan Dreams

1   cup butter, softened
⅓   cup sifted powdered sugar
2   cups all-purpose flour
1   cup chopped pecans
1   teaspoon water
½   teaspoon vanilla extract
½   cup sifted powdered sugar

Combine butter and ⅓ cup powdered sugar in a large bowl. Beat at medium speed of an electric mixer until creamy. Stir in flour, pecans, water, and vanilla, mixing well. Cover and refrigerate dough at least 2 hours.

Roll dough into 1-inch balls, and place on ungreased cookie sheets. Bake at 400° for 8 to 10 minutes. Remove to wire racks to cool slightly. Roll cookies in ½ cup powdered sugar, and cool completely on wire racks. Yield: 4 dozen.

A Picnic Getaway

Setting the Mood

Inside or outside
Picnic basket
Blanket
Portable radio
Plastic dishes
Flowers
Bottle of wine

Menu

Oven-Fried Chicken
Asparagus Vinaigrette
Grapes, Watermelon, Peaches, or Plums
Cheesecake Spread   Crackers

*F*ind a cozy spot, spread a soft quilt, and don't forget the wine. This picnic menu is perfect for a lazy afternoon in the park, perhaps as a prelude to a longer evening together (as the stuffed peppers were for Robert and Francesca) or to rekindle an old relationship. Old-fashioned heart-to-heart conversations, laughing over the good times, and sharing dreams may be all it takes to create a fantastic day for two.

Oven-Fried Chicken

⅓   cup vegetable oil
2½   tablespoons lemon juice
2   tablespoons soy sauce
1½   teaspoons dried parsley flakes
½   teaspoon garlic powder
⅛   teaspoon pepper
2   drops of hot sauce
2   chicken quarters, skinned
¼   cup dry breadcrumbs

Combine first 7 ingredients in a heavy-duty, zip-top plastic bag; add chicken, and seal bag. Place bag in a bowl, squeezing bag gently to blend ingredients. Marinate in refrigerator 4 to 8 hours, turning bag occasionally.

Drain chicken, and discard marinade. Dredge chicken lightly in breadcrumbs. Place chicken on rack in a greased roasting pan; bake, uncovered, at 350° for 40 to 45 minutes or until done. Serve warm or chilled. Yield: 2 servings.

Asparagus Vinaigrette

This vinaigrette works very well with other vegetables like broccoli spears, whole baby carrots, zucchini spears, and cauliflower flowerettes.

½	pound fresh asparagus spears
¼	cup walnut oil
¼	cup cider vinegar
1	tablespoon finely grated fresh Parmesan cheese
1	teaspoon sugar
¼	teaspoon celery salt
¼	teaspoon dry mustard
⅛	teaspoon salt
⅛	teaspoon garlic powder
⅛	teaspoon lemon-pepper seasoning
⅛	teaspoon paprika
2	leaves red tip lettuce
1	tomato, finely diced

Snap off tough ends of asparagus. Remove scales from stalks with a knife or vegetable peeler. Place asparagus in a steamer basket over boiling water. Cover and steam 3 to 5 minutes or until crisp-tender. Rinse with cold water.

Combine oil and next 9 ingredients in a jar; cover tightly, and shake vigorously.

Pour vinaigrette over asparagus; chill 4 hours. Serve on red tip lettuce with diced tomato as a garnish. Yield: 2 servings.

Cheesecake Spread

⌒

*This spread is easily transportable. Simply spoon
cream cheese mixture into a container with a lid; pour preserves
over cream cheese, and cover with lid. Transport it in a cooler,
and remove from cooler 15 minutes before serving.*

½   (8-ounce) package cream cheese, softened
¼   cup unsifted powdered sugar
¼   teaspoon vanilla extract
¼   cup fruit preserves (apricot, strawberry, or raspberry)
Wheat biscuit crackers

Combine cream cheese, powdered sugar, and vanilla, stirring
well. Mound mixture into a ball on a small serving plate. Cover
and chill.

When ready to serve, heat preserves in a small saucepan,
stirring gently, until pourable. Pour preserves over cream cheese
ball. Serve with crackers. Yield: 2 servings.

*Note: This spread can also be made with low-fat or fat-free cream
cheese for a healthier dessert. These types of cream cheese are softer and will
create a less moldable mixture. It may be easiest to serve them from a bowl.*

Have Girlfriends, Will Gossip

When Madge Comes Calling

Setting the Mood

Johnson farmhouse
Pretty dessert plates
Silverware
Antique creamer
Coffeepot

⟁

Menu

Apple Brown Betty
Coffee

*F*ood serves as a pathway to all types of relationships. In the movie, food prompts conversation in the scene between Francesca and Madge, the nosy neighbor. Madge stops by with Apple Brown Betty, using it as a reason to visit and as a disguise for her curiosity about Robert's truck. While this dessert becomes Madge's excuse to snoop, this Betty's even better when shared with more honest intentions and a scoop of vanilla ice cream.

Apple Brown Betty

Betties are baked puddings made of layers of sugared and spiced fruit (usually apple) and breadcrumbs. During the Depression years, many cooks would crumble leftover biscuits to use in this recipe; here we've used graham cracker crumbs instead.

¾	cup firmly packed brown sugar
1	teaspoon ground cinnamon
¼	teaspoon ground nutmeg
¼	teaspoon ground cloves
¼	teaspoon salt
1	teaspoon grated lemon rind
1	teaspoon vanilla extract
2	cups graham cracker crumbs
½	cup butter or margarine, melted
3	medium cooking apples, peeled and sliced (about 3 cups)
3	tablespoons lemon juice, divided
¼	cup water, divided
½	cup raisins, divided (optional)

Whipping cream or vanilla ice cream

Combine brown sugar, cinnamon, nutmeg, cloves, salt, lemon rind, and vanilla; stir until blended, and set aside.

Combine graham cracker crumbs and melted butter. Firmly press ⅔ cup crumb mixture on bottom of a greased 8-inch square pan. Top crumb mixture with half of sliced apples, and sprinkle with half of sugar mixture. Sprinkle 1 tablespoon lemon juice and 2 tablespoons water over top of sugar mixture.

Top with an additional ⅔ cup crumb mixture and, if desired, ¼ cup raisins. Top with remaining apples and remaining sugar mixture. Sprinkle with remaining 2 tablespoons each of lemon juice and water. Top with remaining ¼ cup raisins, if desired, and remaining crumb mixture.

Cover pan with aluminum foil, and bake at 300° for 35 to 40 minutes or until apples are nearly tender. Remove foil, increase heat to 400°, and bake another 10 minutes or until mixture is lightly browned. Serve warm with whipping cream. Yield: 4 to 6 servings.

Behind the Scenes

We call Apple Brown Betty our "interview food."
Just being familiar with this dish secured
the catering job for us. Aware of actress
Meryl Streep's concern for the environment,
we chose to use orchard apples
to prepare this great dessert!

Girls' Lunch Talk

Setting the Mood

Girlfriends
Living area
Luncheon china
Linen napkins
Mimosas, white wine, or bottled waters
Lively music, such as The Supremes
Tulips, snapdragons, or other bright flowers

Menu

Shrimp and Feta Pasta Salad or
Spicy Curried Chicken Salad
Fresh Fruits
Orange-Nut Bread
Bakery Cookies

*T*his menu, like the scene with Madge, can also bridge the way to conversation—this time, perhaps, to a great gab session between girlfriends. The food should stand out anytime friends get together, but it's really secondary to the time shared. These recipes are simple, but spectacular; all you need to add are libations of choice, great background music, and lively conversation. Past promiscuities are always good for a laugh or two.

Shrimp and Feta Pasta Salad

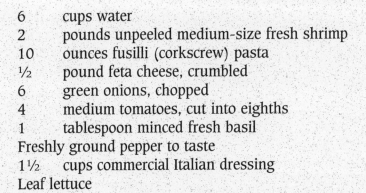

6	cups water
2	pounds unpeeled medium-size fresh shrimp
10	ounces fusilli (corkscrew) pasta
½	pound feta cheese, crumbled
6	green onions, chopped
4	medium tomatoes, cut into eighths
1	tablespoon minced fresh basil

Freshly ground pepper to taste

1½	cups commercial Italian dressing

Leaf lettuce

Bring water to boil; add shrimp, and cook 3 to 5 minutes or until shrimp turn pink. Drain well; rinse with cold water. Chill. Peel shrimp, and devein, if desired.

Cook pasta according to package directions; drain. Rinse with cold water; drain again, and set aside.

Combine shrimp, pasta, feta cheese, and next 5 ingredients, tossing gently. Cover and chill at least 1 hour. Serve on lettuce leaves. Yield: 4 to 6 servings.

Spicy Curried Chicken Salad

1½	pounds skinned, boned chicken breast halves
2	stalks celery, sliced
2	carrots, sliced
1	small onion, quartered
1	teaspoon whole peppercorns
1	bay leaf
½	teaspoon salt
1	sweet red pepper, chopped
1	green pepper, chopped
1	(8-ounce) can sliced water chestnuts, drained
¼	cup minced green onion
¾	cup mayonnaise
1	teaspoon lemon juice
1	to 2 tablespoons curry powder
¼	teaspoon salt

Freshly ground pepper to taste
Dash of hot sauce

Combine first 7 ingredients in a large saucepan; cover with water. Bring to a boil; cover, reduce heat, and simmer 30 minutes or until chicken is done. Drain chicken, discarding flavoring ingredients. Cut chicken into ½-inch pieces. Combine chicken, peppers, water chestnuts, and green onion in a large bowl. Combine mayonnaise, lemon juice, curry powder, salt, pepper, and hot sauce. Spoon over chicken mixture, and toss gently. Yield: 4 to 6 servings.

Orange-Nut Bread

3   cups all-purpose flour
1   cup sugar
1   tablespoon plus 1 teaspoon baking powder
½   teaspoon salt
1   large egg, beaten
¾   cup milk
¾   cup orange juice
¼   cup vegetable oil
2   tablespoons lemon juice
1   teaspoon finely grated orange rind
½   cup chopped pecans
2   tablespoons orange juice
1   teaspoon butter or margarine, melted

Combine first 4 ingredients; make a well in center of mixture. Combine egg, milk, ¾ cup orange juice, oil, and lemon juice. Add to flour mixture, stirring just until moistened. Fold in orange rind and pecans.

Pour batter into a greased 9- x 5- x 3-inch loafpan. Bake at 350° for 1 hour or until a wooden pick inserted in center comes out clean. Cool bread in pan 10 minutes; turn out onto a wire rack.

Prick top of loaf several times with a fork. Combine 2 tablespoons orange juice and butter; spread butter mixture across top of loaf, using a pastry brush. Wrap loaf in aluminum foil, and let cool completely before slicing. Yield: 1 loaf.

A Lifetime of Certainty

A Romantic Dinner

Setting the Mood

Farmhouse dining room
Good dishes
Linen tablecloth and napkins
Yellow candles
Soft blues on the radio
Ranier beer

Menu

Chicken Cacciatore
Steamed Asparagus
Fried Eggplant
Spinach Salad with Strawberries
Spinach Salad Dressing or
Raspberry Vinaigrette
Garlic Bread

The dining room table is set, soft music plays, and Robert lights the candles for their final meal together. But ironically, he and Francesca seem never to eat this meal with its overabundance of food. Their delicious but uneaten dinner symbolizes the anxiety and intensity with which they address the future of their relationship. Eaten or not, food remains the catalyst, the ritual, and the centerpiece through which this relationship develops.

Chicken Cacciatore

2   (5-ounce) skinned, boned chicken breast halves
2   teaspoons olive oil
½   cup chopped onion
1   clove garlic, minced
½   cup tomato sauce
½   teaspoon sugar
½   teaspoon dried basil
½   teaspoon dried oregano
½   teaspoon dried parsley flakes
¼   teaspoon dried rosemary
¼   teaspoon salt
⅛   teaspoon pepper
2   drops of hot sauce
¾   cup chopped tomato
½   cup sliced fresh mushrooms
¼   cup chopped sweet yellow pepper
¼   cup chopped green pepper
¼   cup dry white wine
Hot cooked rice

Brown chicken breasts in hot oil in a large nonstick skillet over
medium heat. Add onion and garlic; cover and cook over low
heat until onion is tender. Stir in tomato sauce and next 8 ingredients. Cover and simmer 15 minutes. Add tomato, mushrooms,
yellow and green peppers, and wine. Simmer 5 to 10 minutes or
until vegetables are tender. Serve over rice or pasta, if desired.
Yield: 2 servings.

Fried Eggplant

This is best when made right at serving time.

¼	cup all-purpose flour
⅛	teaspoon garlic powder
⅛	teaspoon pepper
2	large eggs
¼	cup milk
¾	cup seasoned dry breadcrumbs
1	small eggplant, peeled and sliced ½-inch thick
1	tablespoon basil-flavored oil
1	tablespoon olive oil

Combine flour, garlic powder, and pepper in a shallow bowl. In another bowl, beat eggs and milk together. Spread breadcrumbs on a plate.

Dredge each slice of eggplant in flour mixture, dip into egg mixture, and dredge in breadcrumbs, coating both sides. Heat oils in a large skillet over medium heat. Fry eggplant in batches in hot oil until golden, turning to brown other side and adding additional oil if needed. Keep warm in a 325° oven until all pieces are done, if necessary. Serve immediately. Yield: 2 servings.

Spinach Salad with Strawberries

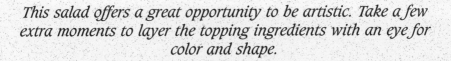

This salad offers a great opportunity to be artistic. Take a few extra moments to layer the topping ingredients with an eye for color and shape.

3	cups loosely packed torn fresh spinach leaves
2	fresh mushrooms, sliced
½	sweet red pepper, cut into thin strips
1	small carrot, peeled and grated
½	small purple onion, thinly sliced
¼	cup crumbled blue cheese (optional)
4	strawberries, sliced
2	tablespoons grated fresh Parmesan cheese
½	cup croutons
2	tablespoons sliced almonds, toasted

Spinach Salad Dressing or Raspberry Vinaigrette
      (following page)

Divide spinach evenly on two salad plates; top evenly with mushrooms and next 8 ingredients. Drizzle with favorite dressing. Yield: 2 servings.

Spinach Salad Dressing

½   cup sugar
1   cup olive oil
½   cup white vinegar
⅓   cup ketchup
2   tablespoons Worcestershire sauce

Combine all ingredients; stir with a wire whisk until blended. Yield: 1¾ cups.

Raspberry Vinaigrette

½   cup walnut oil
¼   cup raspberry vinegar
2   tablespoons raspberry honey
½   teaspoon lemon juice

Combine all ingredients in a small jar; cover tightly, and shake vigorously. Shake again before serving. Yield: ¾ cup.

Note: These ingredients can be found in most gourmet shops.

A Dinner to Remember

Setting the Mood

Inside or outside
Votive candles
Jazz music
Roses
Fine red wine
Linen place mats and napkins
Special card or message tucked in place setting

Menu

Marinated Flank Steak
Mushroom Wild Rice
Sliced Fresh Tomatoes
Fresh Fruit Compote with
Raspberry Sauce
French Vanilla Coffee

Channel any nervous energy about wanting to impress a new date or an old love into the details of planning a perfect evening. Creating an inviting atmosphere is a good place to start. Put extra thought into picking out table linens, selecting a wine that complements the menu, dimming the lights as the evening progresses, and choosing music to match the mood. The effort you take will reflect how much you care.

Marinated Flank Steak

¼   cup olive oil
2   tablespoons red wine vinegar
1   teaspoon dried parsley flakes
1   teaspoon dried marjoram
2   teaspoons Worcestershire sauce
¼   teaspoon salt
¼   teaspoon white pepper
1   clove garlic, crushed
½   pound flank steak

Combine all ingredients except flank steak in a large, heavy-duty, zip-top plastic bag; set bag in a shallow dish, and add steak. Seal bag, and marinate in refrigerator 3 to 8 hours, turning bag occasionally.

    Broil or grill steak 5 minutes per side for medium rare or until meat has reached desired doneness. Cut into thin slices to serve. Yield: 2 servings.

Mushroom Wild Rice

½   cup wild rice
1½   cups beef broth
½   cup dry red wine
2   green onions, thinly sliced
2   tablespoons diced carrot
6   fresh mushrooms, sliced
1   stalk celery, diagonally sliced
1   teaspoon olive oil
¼   cup sliced water chestnuts
1   teaspoon dried parsley flakes
Dash of pepper

Combine rice, beef broth, and wine in a medium saucepan. Bring mixture to a boil over high heat; cover, reduce heat, and simmer 30 minutes.

Sauté onion, carrot, mushrooms, and celery in hot oil 5 minutes in a small saucepan. Add sautéed vegetables, water chestnuts, parsley, and pepper to rice; cover and cook another 15 minutes or until rice is tender. Yield: 2 servings.

Fresh Fruit Compote

This fruit blend (without the Raspberry Sauce) is also delicious as a topping for pound cake or an alternative to the frosting for Yellow Cream Cake (page 106).

4   to 6 strawberries, hulled and quartered
2   kiwifruit, peeled and cubed
½   cup fresh or frozen pineapple chunks
Raspberry Sauce

Combine fruit in individual stemmed wine goblets, and drizzle with Raspberry Sauce. Yield: 2 servings.

Raspberry Sauce

2   pints raspberries or strawberries
2   tablespoons Grand Marnier or other orange-flavored
         liqueur
1   tablespoon superfine sugar

Insert knife blade in food processor bowl; combine raspberries, Grand Marnier, and sugar. Process mixture until blended and smooth. Cover and chill any leftover sauce for another use. Yield: 1½ cups.

Conversation and Comfort Food

Mealtime Nostalgia

Setting the Mood

Farmhouse kitchen
Everyday dishes
Bowl of fresh fruit
Pitcher of sun tea
Overhead lighting
Dessert in front of the television

Menu

Chicken-Fried Steaks
Old-Fashioned Mashed Potatoes with
Country-Style White Gravy
Green Bean Casserole
Drop Biscuits
Molasses Cookies or
Real Butter Cookies

*R*ichard and the children return from the fair and recount their week away. Dutifully, Francesca has a meal prepared, all very comfortably Midwestern, circa 1965 farm fare. Life at the Johnson family farmhouse begins its routine again. Francesca, however, is obviously preoccupied with thoughts of her past few days—thoughts too tangled in her memory to share with anyone.

Chicken-Fried Steaks

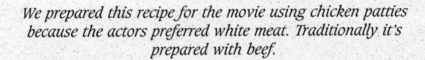

We prepared this recipe for the movie using chicken patties because the actors preferred white meat. Traditionally it's prepared with beef.

⅓   cup all-purpose flour
¼   teaspoon garlic powder
⅛   teaspoon pepper
1   large egg
2   tablespoons milk
4   (4-ounce) ground chicken patties or beef cubed steaks
½   to ¾ cup seasoned dry breadcrumbs
¼   cup vegetable oil

Combine flour, garlic powder, and pepper. Combine egg and milk, beating lightly. Dip chicken patties into flour mixture; then dip in egg mixture, and dredge in breadcrumbs, coating both sides.

Brown patties in hot oil in a large skillet, turning to brown other side. Cover and cook until done, removing lid last 5 minutes to prevent breading from becoming too soft, if desired. Reserve drippings for gravy, if desired. Yield: 4 servings.

Old-Fashioned Mashed Potatoes

For variety, these potatoes are wonderful made with scrubbed, unpeeled potatoes and flavored with garlic, chives, or cheese.

1½   pounds russet potatoes, peeled and cubed
⅓   cup warm milk
2   tablespoons butter or margarine
⅛   teaspoon salt
Dash of pepper
Country-Style White Gravy

Cook potatoes in boiling water to cover 15 minutes or until tender; drain and mash. Add milk and next 3 ingredients; beat with an electric mixer until smooth. Serve with Country-Style White Gravy. Yield: 4 to 6 servings.

Country-Style White Gravy

¼   cup fried meat drippings, including any breading scraps
¼   cup all-purpose flour
2½   cups milk
¼   teaspoon chicken-flavored bouillon granules
Dash of pepper

Combine meat drippings and flour in a large skillet, stirring over medium heat until lightly browned. Gradually stir in milk; cook, stirring constantly, until thickened and bubbly. Stir in bouillon granules and pepper. Yield: 2½ cups.

Green Bean Casserole

Yes, this is the tried-and-true casserole you think it is, and it works as well in the nineties as it did in the sixties.

2   pounds fresh green beans, ends removed, or 2 pounds frozen French-cut green beans, or 2 (14-ounce) cans French-cut green beans
1   (10¾-ounce) can cream of mushroom soup, undiluted
⅛   teaspoon pepper
1   tablespoon cooking sherry
8   medium-size fresh mushrooms, thinly sliced
1   (3-ounce) can French-fried onions

Place fresh green beans in a steamer basket over boiling water. Cover and steam 15 minutes or until crisp-tender. (If using frozen or canned beans, do not steam.)

Combine green beans, soup, pepper, sherry, and mushrooms, stirring gently. Pour into a lightly greased 1¾-quart casserole; top with fried onions. Bake at 350° for 30 minutes, covering casserole with aluminum foil the last 15 minutes to prevent onions from becoming too dark. Yield: 4 to 6 servings.

Drop Biscuits

These little biscuits are great served warm from the oven with butter, margarine, honey, or jam.

2	cups all-purpose flour
2	tablespoons sugar
1	tablespoon plus 1 teaspoon baking powder
½	teaspoon salt
½	cup shortening
1	large egg, beaten
¾	cup milk

Sift together dry ingredients; cut shortening into flour mixture with a pastry blender until mixture resembles coarse meal. Combine egg and milk; add to flour mixture, stirring until dry ingredients are moistened. Drop dough by rounded tablespoonfuls onto a lightly greased baking sheet. Bake at 450° for 8 minutes or until biscuits are golden brown. Yield: 1½ dozen.

Molasses Cookies

2³⁄₄   cups all-purpose flour
1   tablespoon ground ginger
2   teaspoons baking soda
1   teaspoon ground cinnamon
¹⁄₂   teaspoon salt
³⁄₄   cup butter
1¹⁄₂   cups sugar, divided
1   large egg
¹⁄₂   cup molasses

In a bowl, combine flour, ginger, baking soda, cinnamon, and salt. Set aside.

In a large saucepan, heat butter until melted; gradually add 1 cup sugar. Mix well. Beat in egg and molasses. Remove from heat. Add flour mixture, ¹⁄₂ cup at a time, until all the flour is mixed into the molasses mixture. Let mixture cool until it begins to thicken. Place remaining sugar in a bowl. Drop dough by rounded teaspoonfuls into sugar and coat all sides; place on an ungreased cookie sheet. Bake at 350° for 6 to 8 minutes or until slightly puffy and edges are set. Transfer to a plate, and cover with plastic wrap while warm to keep soft texture. Yield: 3¹⁄₂ dozen.

Real Butter Cookies

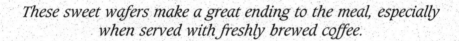

These sweet wafers make a great ending to the meal, especially when served with freshly brewed coffee.

1	pound butter, softened
1	cup sugar
2	large eggs
2½	tablespoons milk
1	teaspoon vanilla extract
½	teaspoon almond extract
4	cups all-purpose flour
½	teaspoon baking soda
½	teaspoon cream of tartar
⅛	teaspoon salt

Beat butter at medium speed of an electric mixer until soft and creamy. Gradually add sugar, beating well. Add eggs, one at a time, beating after each addition. Add milk and flavorings, beating until blended.

Combine flour, soda, cream of tartar, and salt, stirring until blended. Stir into butter mixture. Drop dough by rounded teaspoonfuls onto ungreased cookie sheets. Grease and flour bottom of a glass, and use glass to flatten each cookie. Bake at 350° for 10 to 12 minutes or until very lightly browned on the edges. Yield: 5 dozen.

A Menu for Memories

Setting the Mood

Dining room
Rich fall-colored linens
Soft vocal or instrumental background music
Slightly dimmed lights
Mums
Childhood stories
Memorabilia

Menu

Vegetable-Stuffed Pork Loin
Roasted New Potatoes
Fresh Corn on the Cob or
Steamed Broccoli
Romaine-Blue Cheese Salad
Swedish Rye Bread

For occasions of reminiscence and nostalgia with your own family, try these recipes. They're sure to become the "comfort foods" of the next generation. Schedule enough time to linger over the meal and to enjoy comfortable conversation. And don't hesitate to move into the family room and drag out home movies and vacation photos after the last bite. The dishes can wait. This is family.

Vegetable-Stuffed Pork Loin

⌒

½   cup finely chopped onion
¼   cup finely chopped celery
¼   cup finely chopped carrot
4   fresh mushrooms, chopped
1½   tablespoons butter or margarine, divided
¼   cup chopped pecans
1   cup seasoned, dry breadcrumbs
½   cup water
¼   cup red wine vinegar
1   tablespoon chopped fresh parsley
1   teaspoon beef-flavored bouillon granules
¼   teaspoon pepper
2   pounds boneless pork loin roast
1   tablespoon browning-and-seasoning sauce

Sauté onion, celery, carrot, and mushrooms in 1½ teaspoons butter in a skillet until onions are tender. Stir in pecans, breadcrumbs, water, vinegar, parsley, bouillon granules, and pepper.

Preheat oven to 375°. Using a long, sharp knife, make a vertical slit from one end of roast to other, cutting almost to, but not through, bottom. Make a horizontal slit through roast to create a "+" opening for stuffing.

Spoon small quantities of breadcrumb mixture at a time into one end of the roast. Continue to add stuffing until visible from other end. Firmly press stuffing from both ends toward center of roast, adding any extra stuffing that will fit. Place roast in a greased 11- x 7- x 1½-inch casserole; spoon any remaining stuffing around roast.

Melt remaining 1 tablespoon of butter; add seasoning sauce. Brush top of roast with half of butter mixture. Place roast in oven; reduce temperature to 325°. Bake 40 minutes; baste with remaining butter mixture. Cover roast with aluminum foil, and bake an additional 35 minutes or until done. Remove roast from oven, slice with a sharp knife, and arrange in a spiral pattern on a serving platter; spoon any extra stuffing on the side. Yield: 4 to 6 servings.

Behind the Scenes

As we were leaving the movie set one day, a tall, mysterious Robert Kincaid dressed in jeans and an army-green shirt approached us. It was Clint Eastwood—and this was our moment! We exchanged warm handshakes and spoke briefly. A simple moment, but one of our great memories.

Roasted New Potatoes

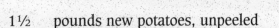

1½	pounds new potatoes, unpeeled
1½	tablespoons olive oil
1	teaspoon salt
¼	teaspoon paprika
¼	teaspoon dried rosemary
⅛	teaspoon pepper
1	clove garlic, crushed

Place potatoes in a steamer basket over boiling water. Cover and steam 5 to 8 minutes or until slightly tender. Cut potatoes in half or into wedges, if desired, and place potatoes in a lightly greased 13- x 9- x 2-inch pan.

Combine oil, salt, paprika, rosemary, pepper, and garlic; brush potatoes with oil mixture. Bake at 375° for 10 minutes or until tender and browned, stirring occasionally. Yield: 4 to 6 servings.

Romaine-Blue Cheese Salad

1	large head romaine lettuce
1	cup red seedless grapes, halved
1	Granny Smith apple, diced
½	cup diagonally sliced celery
1	cup safflower oil
½	cup sugar
3	tablespoons grated onion
2	teaspoons celery seeds
1	teaspoon dry mustard
1	teaspoon salt
4	leaves red tip lettuce
½	cup chopped walnuts, toasted
½	cup crumbled blue cheese
1	cup seasoned croutons

Combine romaine, grapes, apple, and celery in a small bowl; set aside.

Combine oil, sugar, onion, celery seeds, mustard, and salt. Stir with a wire whisk until blended.

Spoon salad mixture evenly onto four salad plates lined with red tip lettuce. Sprinkle salads evenly with walnuts, blue cheese, and croutons. Drizzle dressing over each salad. Yield: 4 to 6 servings.

Swedish Rye Bread

1   package active dry yeast
2   cups warm water (105° to 115°), divided
⅓   cup molasses
¼   cup butter or margarine, softened
2   cups rye flour
3   tablespoons brown sugar
1   tablespoon honey
1½   teaspoons salt
3½   to 4 cups all-purpose flour
Butter or margarine

Combine yeast and 2 tablespoons warm water in a large bowl; let stand 5 minutes. Stir in remaining water, molasses, ¼ cup butter, rye flour, brown sugar, honey, and salt; beat at medium speed of an electric mixer until blended. Gradually stir in enough all-purpose flour to make a soft dough.

Turn dough onto a well-floured surface, and knead until smooth and elastic (approximately 5 minutes). Place dough in a greased bowl, turning to grease top. Cover and let rise in a warm spot (85°), free from drafts, 1 hour or until doubled in bulk.

Punch dough down. Divide in half, and place in two greased 9- x 5- x 3-inch loafpans. Cover and let dough rise in pans 30 minutes. Uncover and bake at 325° for 40 to 45 minutes or until bread is golden and sounds hollow when tapped. Brush with additional butter. Cool on wire racks. Yield: 2 loaves.

By Popular Demand

Blue Plate Special

Setting the Mood

Farmhouse kitchen
Everyday dishes
Bottle of ketchup on the table
Basket of freshly picked tomatoes
Radio in background

Menu

Brown Sugar Meat Loaf
Homestyle au Gratin Potatoes
Creamed Peas and Onions or
Broiled Tomatoes
Waldorf Salad
Country Cornbread

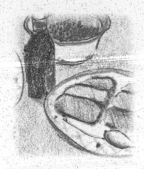

*R*ichard asks Francesca to prepare his favorite Brown Sugar Meat Loaf for dinner one evening after returning from the fair. His request comes during one of her toughest emotional times, as she struggles with her decision to stay with her family and forego the completeness she fantasizes about with Robert. Even so, her sense of responsibility helps her carry out Richard's dinner request. With regard to leaving, there are simply too many people, too many circumstances, and too many emotions in her life to simply walk away. Better she stay and do what it takes to be happy.

Brown Sugar Meat Loaf

For the movie, we prepared this meat loaf using ground turkey instead of beef because the actors preferred white meat.

2	pounds ground round
1	cup herb-seasoned stuffing mix
¼	cup chopped onion
⅛	teaspoon salt
⅛	teaspoon pepper
2	large eggs, lightly beaten
¾	cup milk
2	tablespoons commercial barbecue sauce
Vegetable cooking spray	
¼	cup ketchup
2	tablespoons brown sugar
1	teaspoon dry mustard

Combine ground round, stuffing mix, onion, salt, and pepper. Beat eggs, milk, and barbecue sauce; add to meat mixture, mixing well. Press mixture into a 9- x 5- x 3-inch loafpan sprayed with cooking spray. Combine ketchup, brown sugar, and mustard; spread over top of meat loaf. Bake, uncovered, at 350° for 1 hour and 30 minutes or until a thermometer inserted in center of loaf registers 160°. Remove from loafpan immediately. Yield: 6 servings.

Homestyle au Gratin Potatoes

½   cup chopped onion
¼   cup butter or margarine, melted
½   cup all-purpose flour
1   cup milk
1   cup half-and-half
1   (8-ounce) carton sour cream
1   cup (4 ounces) shredded American cheese
1   teaspoon salt
⅛   teaspoon white pepper
1   teaspoon chopped chives
5   large russet potatoes, unpeeled and sliced ⅛-inch thick

Sauté onion in butter in a large skillet until tender. Add flour, stirring until smooth. Cook 1 minute, stirring constantly. Gradually add milk and half-and-half; cook over medium heat, stirring constantly, until thickened and bubbly. Add sour cream, cheese, salt, pepper, and chives, stirring until cheese melts.

Layer half of potatoes in a lightly greased 13- x 9- x 2-inch baking dish. Top potatoes with half of cheese sauce. Cover with remaining potatoes, followed by remaining cheese sauce. Cover with aluminum foil, and bake at 350° for 45 minutes. Uncover and continue to bake 30 to 40 more minutes or until potatoes are tender. Yield: 6 servings.

Creamed Peas and Onions

2	tablespoons butter or margarine, divided
1½	tablespoons all-purpose flour
1	cup milk
¼	teaspoon salt
⅛	teaspoon white pepper
⅛	teaspoon dried dillweed
2	(10-ounce) packages frozen English peas
½	cup drained, canned pearl onions
½	cup soft breadcrumbs

Melt 1 tablespoon butter in a large saucepan; add flour, stirring until smooth. Cook 1 minute, stirring constantly. Gradually add milk; cook over medium heat, stirring constantly, until thickened and bubbly. Add salt, pepper, and dillweed. Gently fold in peas and onions. Pour into a lightly greased 1½-quart casserole.

Melt remaining 1 tablespoon butter; add breadcrumbs, and toss gently. Sprinkle on top of peas. Bake, uncovered, at 350° for 15 minutes or until bubbly. Yield: 6 servings.

Broiled Tomatoes

~~~

6	vine-ripened homegrown tomatoes
⅛	teaspoon salt
⅛	teaspoon freshly ground pepper
¾	cup Italian-seasoned breadcrumbs
¼	cup plus 2 tablespoons grated fresh Parmesan cheese
1	tablespoon chopped fresh parsley
3	tablespoons butter or margarine, melted

Wash tomatoes, and slice off tops to remove each core. Cut a small slice from bottom of tomatoes to make them stand flat. Sprinkle top of each tomato with salt and pepper. Place on heavy-duty aluminum foil on a baking sheet. Broil tomatoes 5½-inches from heat for 3 minutes.

Combine breadcrumbs, cheese, and parsley; toss with butter. Spread crumb mixture evenly on each tomato. Broil 5 minutes or until crumbs have browned and cheese has melted. Serve immediately. Yield: 6 servings.

Waldorf Salad

If you're partial to raisins in your Waldorf Salad, feel free to add as many as you like.

1	(8-ounce) carton vanilla yogurt
1	tablespoon sugar
2	tablespoons orange juice
½	teaspoon grated lemon rind

Dash of ground red pepper
Dash of ground cinnamon

1	red apple, cored and chopped
1	green apple, cored and chopped
½	cup red seedless grapes, halved
½	cup sliced celery
¼	cup chopped pecans, toasted

Combine yogurt, sugar, orange juice, lemon rind, red pepper, and cinnamon in a large bowl, mixing well. Add apples, grapes, and celery, tossing gently. Spoon into a serving bowl, and sprinkle with pecans. Yield: 4 to 6 servings.

Country Cornbread

1   cup cornmeal
1   cup all-purpose flour
¼   cup sugar
2   teaspoons baking powder
½   teaspoon baking soda
½   teaspoon salt
1½   cups buttermilk
¼   cup vegetable oil
1   large egg, lightly beaten

Grease a 10-inch cast-iron skillet or an 8-inch square pan. Place pan in a 425° oven 2 minutes or until hot.

Combine cornmeal, flour, sugar, baking powder, soda, and salt in a bowl. Combine buttermilk, oil, and egg; pour oil mixture over cornmeal mixture, and stir just until dry ingredients are moistened.

Pour batter into prepared skillet. Bake at 425° for 20 minutes or until cornbread pulls slightly away from edge of pan. Serve warm with butter and honey. Yield: 6 to 8 servings.

An Easy Feast for Friends

Setting the Mood

Good friends
Living area or patio
Fireplace or citronella candles
Upbeat music, such as The Temptations
Jazzy cocktail napkins and disposable plates
Libations of choice

Menu

Baked Brie in a Bread Bowl or
White Cheddar Cheese Balls
Shredded Chicken Sandwiches or
Chilled Shrimp Bowl with Cocktail Sauce
Lahvosh Pizzas
Vegetable Relishes with
Fat Sauce or Dill Dip
Fresh Grapes and Strawberries

*F*riends are synonymous with great times, and it's easy to make them happy with this appetizer feast. Its long list of simple recipes makes for easy entertaining. Just mix and match them based on your food preferences and the number of people you invite, and prepare what you can ahead of time. Then relax, turn up the music, and enjoy the company as soon as the doorbell rings.

Baked Brie in a Bread Bowl

2	cups water
1	cup sliced almonds
1½	tablespoons sugar

Vegetable cooking spray

4	(6-inch) pita bread rounds
2	cloves garlic, minced
½	cup olive oil
1	(16- to 20-ounce) round loaf Vienna bread or butter crust bread
1½	pounds Brie cheese

Bring water to a boil in a small saucepan. Add almonds, and boil 1 minute; drain. Toss almonds with sugar, and spread in a thin layer on a baking sheet lightly coated with cooking spray. Bake at 350° for 5 to 7 minutes or until lightly browned; let cool. (These will crisp as they cool.)

Cut each bread round into 8 wedges; slice top and bottom pieces apart. Spread on an ungreased baking sheet. Combine garlic and oil; brush bread lightly with oil mixture. Bake at 350° for 6 to 8 minutes or until toasted.

Cut a circle in top of bread loaf, leaving a ¾-inch edge. Scoop out center of bread to make a 2½-inch deep well, leaving the bottom intact. Brush inside of loaf lightly with remaining oil mixture. Cut rind from cheese, and cut cheese into chunks; place cheese in center of bread. Bake at 350° for 15 to 20 minutes or until cheese is melted. To serve, place bread bowl on a tray; sprinkle with almonds, and surround with pita chips. Serve immediately. Yield: 12 to 15 appetizer servings.

White Cheddar Cheese Balls

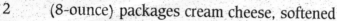

2	(8-ounce) packages cream cheese, softened
2	cups (8 ounces) shredded New York white Cheddar cheese
2	tablespoons thinly sliced green onion
½	teaspoon garlic powder

Combine cream cheese and Cheddar cheese in a large bowl, mixing until blended. Add green onion and garlic powder, mixing well; cover and chill until firm.

Roll cheese mixture into bite-size balls, and serve as desired. Yield: 3 dozen.

Serving options:

- Roll half the balls in 2 tablespoons paprika and half in 2 tablespoons chopped fresh parsley.
- Roll in ½ cup ground almonds or pecans.
- Serve in a lipped dish on a bed of 1 cup salsa.
- Serve on a bed of 1 cup mango chutney.
- Serve plain on a platter with decorative wooden picks.

Shredded Chicken Sandwiches

4	skinned, boned chicken breast halves (1¼ pounds)
¼	small onion, cut into very thin slices
½	cup chicken broth
1	tablespoon cornstarch
½	cup dry white wine, divided
2	tablespoons teriyaki sauce
2	teaspoons lemon juice
2	tablespoons molasses
2	tablespoons brown mustard

Dash of ground ginger
Dash of dried parsley flakes

8	silver dollar-size cocktail buns, toasted

Place chicken in a saucepan; cover with water, and bring to a boil. Boil 5 minutes; remove from heat, and let stand another 5 minutes. Transfer to a plate to cool. When cool, shred.

Meanwhile, steam onion in chicken broth in a saucepan over medium-low heat for 10 minutes. Combine cornstarch and just enough wine to make a thin paste; set aside. Add remaining wine, teriyaki sauce, lemon juice, molasses, and mustard to the onion strips. Stir in shredded chicken until evenly coated. Add cornstarch paste, and stir over low heat until sauce has thickened. Add ginger and parsley. Cook until chicken is heated through. Serve on toasted cocktail buns. Yield: approximately 2 cups (enough for 8 small sandwiches).

Note: If miniature buns are unavailable, use toasted French bread rolls skewered with frill toothpicks and cut into wedges.

Chilled Shrimp Bowl

6   cups water
2   tablespoons salt
2   bay leaves
1   lemon, halved
2   pounds unpeeled jumbo fresh shrimp
Crushed ice
Cocktail Sauce (following page)
4   sprigs fresh parsley
Lemon and lime wedges

Combine first 4 ingredients in a Dutch oven, and bring to a boil. Add shrimp, and cook 3 to 5 minutes or until shrimp turn pink. Drain well, and discard seasonings; rinse shrimp with cold water. Chill.

To serve, fill a large bowl or serving dish with ice, fitting a smaller bowl for sauce into the center. Place shrimp on top of ice around outside edge of sauce bowl. Fill sauce bowl with Cocktail Sauce. Garnish with fresh parsley and lemon and lime wedges. Provide a small bowl for discarded tails. Yield: 6 to 8 servings.

Cocktail Sauce

~~~~~~

2	cups chili sauce
⅓	cup Worcestershire sauce
¼	cup fresh lemon juice
2	tablespoons prepared horseradish
2	teaspoons finely chopped onion
2	cloves garlic, minced
½	teaspoon pepper
⅛	to ¼ teaspoon hot sauce

Combine all ingredients; mix well. Cover and chill at least 1 hour.
Yield: 2½ cups.

Greek Lahvosh

This easy pizza is perfect for a toga theme party—just have plenty of ouzo (a Greek liqueur), olives, and sheets on hand.

1   (16-inch) lahvosh cracker (or several small lahvosh crackers to serve individually)
1   tablespoon olive oil
2   cups coarsely chopped fresh spinach leaves
1   cup crumbled feta cheese
2   cloves garlic, crushed
2   small tomatoes, thinly sliced
1   cup (4 ounces) shredded mozzarella cheese

Place lahvosh on a large baking sheet, and brush with olive oil; top with spinach. Combine feta cheese and garlic; sprinkle feta mixture over spinach. Top with sliced tomato; sprinkle with mozzarella cheese. Bake at 350° for 10 to 15 minutes or until cheese is lightly browned. Ask guests to break off portions. Yield: 6 to 8 appetizer servings.

Note: Lahvosh is a Middle Eastern cracker bread available in various shapes and sizes in most grocery stores.

Islander Lahvosh

Create a seaside atmosphere with tiki torches, reggae music, and daiquiris.

1	(16-inch) lahvosh cracker (or several small lahvosh crackers to serve individually)
4	ounces tiny whole frozen, cooked shrimp, thawed
4	ounces prosciutto, thinly sliced
1	(8-ounce) can artichoke hearts, drained and halved
¼	cup sliced ripe olives
¼	cup diced sun-dried tomato
2	tablespoons basil olive oil
1	clove garlic, crushed
1	cup (4 ounces) shredded mozzarella cheese
½	cup grated shredded fresh Parmesan cheese

Place lahvosh on a large baking sheet. Layer shrimp, prosciutto, artichoke hearts, olives, and dried tomato on top. Combine olive oil and garlic; drizzle over tomatoes. Top with mozzarella and Parmesan cheeses. Bake at 350° for 10 to 15 minutes or until cheese is lightly browned. Ask guests to break off desired portions. Yield: 6 to 8 appetizer servings.

Note: Chopped sun-dried tomatoes are available marinated in oil; if using these, omit the olive oil and garlic from the recipe.

Fiesta Lahvosh

Plan a south-of-the-border theme with piñatas, margaritas, and castanets.

1	(16-inch) lahvosh cracker (or several small lahvosh crackers to serve individually)
1	cup canned refried beans
1⅓	cups shredded cooked chicken breast (about 8 ounces)
1	cup salsa
2	tablespoons chopped fresh cilantro
1½	cups (6 ounces) shredded mozzarella cheese

Place lahvosh on a large baking sheet, and spread with refried beans. Top with shredded chicken and salsa; sprinkle with cilantro. Top with mozzarella cheese. Bake at 350° for 10 to 15 minutes or until cheese is lightly browned. Ask guests to break off desired portions. Yield: 6 to 8 appetizer servings.

Fat Sauce

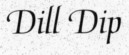

1	(16-ounce) carton sour cream or plain yogurt
2	tablespoons Worcestershire sauce
1	tablespoon chopped fresh parsley
¼	teaspoon seasoned salt
⅛	teaspoon celery salt

Dash of chili powder

2	drops of hot sauce

Combine all ingredients in a small bowl; stir well. Cover and chill. Use as a dip for fresh vegetables. Yield: 2 cups.

Dill Dip

1	(16-ounce) carton sour cream or plain yogurt
¼	cup buttermilk
2½	teaspoons dried dillweed
½	teaspoon paprika
½	teaspoon lemon-pepper seasoning
½	teaspoon dried parsley flakes
½	teaspoon dried onion flakes

Dash of salt

Combine all ingredients in a small bowl; stir well. Cover mixture and chill. Serve with fresh vegetables. Yield: 2¼ cups.

Gifts from the Kitchen

A Cake from the Heart

Setting the Mood
Lucy Redfield's front porch
Simple serving platter

Menu

Yellow Cream Cake with Buttercream Frosting
Coffee

*I*n one of the film's final scenes, Francesca takes a cake to Lucy Redfield, a local woman regarded as more promiscuous than Winterset, Iowa's 1965 norm. As soon as word about Lucy spreads through town, many of her friends shun her. But as a result of Francesca's encounter with Robert, she becomes empathetic to Lucy and initiates their friendship with this cake. It marks the beginning of a beautiful and lifelong bond.

Yellow Cream Cake

—————⌒—————

½	cup butter, softened
1½	cups sugar
4	egg yolks
2¾	cups all-purpose flour
2½	teaspoons baking powder
½	teaspoon salt
1¼	cups milk
2	teaspoons vanilla extract

Buttercream Frosting (following page)

Beat butter at medium speed of an electric mixer until creamy; gradually add sugar, beating well. Add egg yolks, one at a time, beating after each addition.

Combine flour, baking powder, and salt; add to butter mixture alternately with milk, beginning and ending with flour mixture. Mix at low speed at least 1 minute after each addition until blended. Stir in vanilla. Pour batter into 2 greased and floured 9-inch round cakepans.

Bake at 350° for 25 to 30 minutes or until a wooden pick inserted in center comes out clean. Cool in pans on wire racks 10 minutes; remove from pans, and let cool completely on wire racks. Spread Buttercream Frosting between layers and on top and sides of cake. Yield: one 2-layer cake.

Buttercream Frosting

¼	cup butter, softened
1	(16-ounce) package powdered sugar, sifted
1	teaspoon vanilla extract
2	to 4 tablespoons hot water
½	(8-ounce) container frozen whipped topping, thawed

Beat butter at medium speed of an electric mixer until creamy.
Add powdered sugar and vanilla; gradually add hot water, beating at low speed until mixture is smooth and creamy. Gently fold
in whipped topping, and immediately spread frosting on cake.
Cover and chill until ready to serve. Yield: 3 cups.

Behind the Scenes

*What we thought would make a simple food
assignment, Yellow Cake, turned into a prop
that had to meet many movie-making
requirements—lighting, placement, size, color,
and on and on. Details are everything.
Yours need not be so complicated.*

A Friendly Gesture

Setting the Mood

Friend's house
Gift platter
Card

Menu

Apricot Coffee Crescents

A gesture of friendship, like Francesca's cake for Lucy, can be a physical expression of caring. These Apricot Coffee Crescents are a thoughtful way to send your sentiments to a friend. Place your creation on an attractive disposable platter, perhaps including an accompaniment of flavored coffee for a gourmet cook or a neighborhood address list for a newcomer. Add a ribbon and a card, and you've made someone's day.

Apricot Coffee Crescents

You can vary the filling in these pastries by adding favorite fruit or nut combinations.

2	packages active dry yeast
¼	cup warm water (105° to 115°)
4	cups all-purpose flour
1	teaspoon salt
1	tablespoon sugar
1	cup butter or margarine
3	large eggs, separated
1	cup milk
2	(16-ounce) packages dried apricots
1½	cups sugar, divided
1½	cups sifted powdered sugar
2	to 3 tablespoons water
½	cup sliced almonds, toasted

Combine yeast and warm water in a small bowl, and let stand 5 minutes.

Combine flour, salt, and 1 tablespoon sugar in a large bowl. Cut in butter with a pastry blender until mixture resembles coarse meal. Combine egg yolks and milk; beat lightly, and stir into dough. Add yeast mixture to dough, stirring until blended. Cover and refrigerate at least 4 hours.

Put apricots in a saucepan; add water to cover. Cover and cook apricots over medium heat 15 to 20 minutes or until plumped, adding water as needed. Drain off any excess water. Stir in ½ cup sugar. Divide apricots into four equal portions.

Beat egg whites at high speed of an electric mixer until foamy. Gradually add remaining 1 cup sugar, 1 tablespoon at a time, beating until stiff peaks form and sugar dissolves.

Divide dough into 4 equal portions. Roll one portion of dough into a 12-inch round on heavily floured wax paper. (Keep remaining dough refrigerated.) Spread one-fourth of the egg white mixture over dough, spreading to ¼ inch from edges. Spread one-fourth portion of apricot mixture on half of egg white mixture. Fold untopped side of dough over apricots (using wax paper to support dough as it's folded); seal and flute edges of dough.

Transfer pastry to a greased baking sheet; shape into a crescent. Cut slits in top crust. Repeat process with remaining dough and filling. Do not allow dough to rise. Bake at 350° for 25 minutes or until golden. Cool on wire racks.

Combine powdered sugar and enough water to form a thin icing; drizzle over crescents. Sprinkle with toasted almonds. Yield: 4 coffee cakes.

Index

METRIC MEASURE CONVERSIONS

When You Know...	Multiply by... Mass (weight)	To Find Approximate...	Symbol
ounces	28	grams	g
pounds	0.45	kilograms	kg
	(volume)		
teaspoons	5	milliliters	ml
tablespoons	15	milliliters	ml
fluid ounces	30	milliliters	ml
cups	0.24	liters	l
pints	0.47	liters	l
quarts	0.95	liters	l
gallons	3.8	liters	l

METRIC MEASURE EQUIVALENTS

Cup Measure	Volume (Liquid)	Solid (Butter)	Fine Powder (Flour)	Granular (Sugar)	Grain (Rice)
1	250 ml	200 g	140 g	190 g	150 g
¾	188 ml	150 g	105 g	143 g	113 g
⅔	167 ml	133 g	93 g	127 g	100 g
½	125 ml	100 g	70 g	95 g	75 g
⅓	83 ml	67 g	47 g	63 g	50 g
¼	63 ml	50 g	35 g	48 g	38 g
⅛	31 ml	25 g	18 g	24 g	19 g